Back to Basics
An Awareness Primer

Nancy Spence
InnerVision / Bryson City, NC

Published by:

InnerVision
Guided Introspection

9400 Hwy 19 West
Bryson City, NC 28713

For a schedule of InnerVision workshops and seminars, or if you are interested in bringing one to your area, please write to the address above, or call (704) 488-6754 or (800) 298-8209.

@ 1995 by Nancy Spence

All rights reserved
including the right of reproduction
in whole or in any form.

First Edition 1995

Layout by Family Features, Shawnee Mission, KS.
Graphic designs by Laura Paulus and Nancy Spence.

Printing and binding by The Mazer Corporation.

ISBN 0-9643818-0-X

DEDICATION

To the Vichara Roshi
who still teaches my heart,

and to the
Shasta Abbey sangha

ACKNOWLEDGEMENTS

In gratitude to:

Jane Edwards, *my partner: You have become a world of happiness and celebration for me. I can imagine no other place for my heart.*

Cheri Huber: *my Dharma friend for 22 years.*

Jan Letendre: *InnerVision friend whose courage and willingness are an inspiration and resource for me.*

Beetle, Emily, *and* **Frances Barbour; Jackie Irene; Christa Rypins; Penny Scheller; June Shiver:** *for love, support, encouragement, and ideas.*

Mary Ellen Hammond, Sara Jenkins, Jim Parham *and* **Marie Fulmer Turner:** *for support, encouragement and technical assistance.*

All InnerVision facilitators, *past and present, from North Carolina and California, who seek to learn from these skills.*

Mike Perkins, Laura Paulus, *and* **Marsha Valentine** *of Family Features who make graphics and layout fun!*

Table of Contents

How To Use This Workbook	vi
Chapter 1 - Projection	1
Flowers in a Vase	2
Picture	9
Toy Animal or Pet	12
The Mall	14
A Friend	16
A Friend and the Mall	17
Some Reading	18
Interim Session on Centering	21
Chapter 2 - Postures	24
Postures Exposé	25
Levels and Degrees of Postures	32
Postures Identification	34
Major Messages	38
Interim Session on Centering	42
Chapter 3 - Subpersonalities	44
Discovering Subpersonalities	45
The Bus	52
Alone on a Hill	56
Listening to Your Subpersonalities	60
Interim Session on Centering	66
Chapter 4 - Disidentification	68
Letting Go	69
Speaking in the third Person	73
And Then (S)He...	74
Final Session on Centering	76
Epilogue	77
Glossary of Terms	78
Further Reading	79

HOW TO USE THIS WORKBOOK:

The introspective skills dealt with in this book seem to develop naturally in the progression presented here, and for that reason, I encourage you to work through the sessions in order. But however you determine to proceed through the book, give yourself the opportunity to experience all it offers by doing each exercise fully, completely, with your heart open. Write as much as you can when writing is suggested. Involve a friend's support from the beginning if this feels good to you. (Several times you will be asked to include a friend in an exercise.) Of course, you may find that this workbook does not suit you. In that case, I hope you will be accepting of yourself and your own inclination - that you will choose loving yourself over any postures about "completing what you start."

The audiocassette tape that accompanies this workbook contains exercises in centering and guided imagery. Together, the tape and the text provide experiences that open the awareness, while the workbook is designed to stimulate responses to these experiences - questions, insights, conclusions, expansions of the ideas presented. Space is left after each item for you to write in your responses, and the lefthand pages are blank so that they can be used as well.

When you get to the last page of the book, you might start over again. You will be surprised how different the exercises and skills look the second time - or third, or fourth, or fifth. I have been doing these exercises for 18 years, and I learn new things about myself every time.

Chapter 1

Projection

SESSION ONE

Here is what you will need to complete this session:
- 1 hour of uninterrupted time
- Pages 2-8 of this workbook
- Something with which to write
- Several flowers in a vase

Centering Yourself: Play the first centering exercise on the centering tape, following the suggestions given. Then write down any realizations and awarenesses you had while doing the centering.

First Exercise:
Sit quietly and look at the flowers in the vase. For several minutes, just look at the flowers you have there with you.

In the space provided, begin to write as if you are the flowers. You will be writing in the first person; that is, you will write, "I see..., I think..., I feel..., etc." Just let yourself begin to write from the perspective of the flowers. It might be helpful to look up occasionally at the flowers as you write.

Be sure to take the time to complete this writing before you continue with the next exercise.

Second Exercise:
    Think of an acquaintance you have made recently but do not know very well yet. When you have thought of someone, write down three words or phrases you would use to describe this new acquaintance to another person. Your phrases may or may not include a physical description. There is no right or wrong here - just three words or phrases you would use to describe this new acquaintance to a third person. This time, write your words or phrases in the third person. An example might be: "Emily is bright, has a quick sense of humor and is sensitive."

Write your three words or phrases on the blanks below.

_____, _____, & _____

Now, read these out loud, using the person's name.

_____, is
(Person's name)

_____, _____, & _____.

    After you complete the two exercises above, read the following description of the activities you have been doing. It might be helpful to read it several times.

What you have been experiencing in the two exercises, the one with the flowers and the one in which you listed three qualities of someone else, is an introspective process known as PROJECTION.

We humans are an ongoing experience of sensory stimulation. Light, color, sounds, smells, tastes, and tactile stimulations are happening around and within us every second. These ongoing stimulations, with their resulting thoughts and emotions (internal stimuli) are the filters through which we experience, project, and then interpret the world. When we look at someone and think we know what is going on with her, we are projecting onto that person from what is going on (or has gone on) with us. We are projecting from our own experience of our world. Maybe this thing is not happening to us this very minute; however, we have had the experience within us or we could not "see" it anywhere else.

In truth, we cannot "see" anything "out there" that is not our own experience. We know the experience within ourselves first, or we could not see it in other places, things or persons.

Now you are going to own the three qualities you gave to the new acquaintance - since you saw them, they are in you - by rewriting them. This time, use an "I" statement. Be sure to use the very same words or phrases, adding or taking away nothing.

"I am _____, _____, & _____.

After you write these three words or phrases, say them out loud.

"I am _____, _____, & _____.

Sit still with what you have just done for a minute or so. Become aware of how you feel as you do this. How do you manifest these same three qualities you gave away to your new acquaintance? Can you admit to yourself that you have these qualities? Take a few moments to respond to these questions in the space provided.

Some of us are uncomfortable owning the qualities we think we see in others - it is difficult for us to admit that we have certain qualities. For others of us, it is a great relief to own these projections as our own, and to stop pretending we can be accurate in perceiving what is going on with someone else. Often we experience joy as we realize how the wonderful loving qualities we happily give to others are first inside ourselves.

When you are working to own these qualities, it is helpful to realize that perhaps it is true Emily is bright, has a quick sense of humor and is sensitive. Just because you are projecting does not mean your projections are untrue. Yet what you can begin to see is that Emily is intelligent in ways you value for yourself. She thinks the same things are funny that you do; she makes others laugh in ways you can; she sees the lighter side in ways you appreciate; she is sensitive in ways you are sensitive, and to similar situations. You may not be aware of these qualities in yourself now, yet you have them and the experience of them, no matter how well hidden from your awareness at the moment. You could not recognize them in Emily if this were not so. You have to go inside (to your own experience) to project outside and label something or someone.

Projection can be difficult to stay focused upon as it often goes against all our conditioning. We are brought up to focus away from our own qualities; many of us are conditioned to believe self-awareness is selfish. Instead, we unconsciously project our own qualities onto others, especially children and animals. Yet consider this: I take my dog everywhere with me - to work, running, vacations and short trips to the store. I bought a pickup with a camper shell so she can ride with me, and even padded it with carpet. Why? Because she likes to go with me? Because she enjoys running and vacations? Because she looks sad when I leave her at home? Maybe this is her experience. But one thing I know for sure: it is certainly my experience. I hate leaving her. I feel sad. I love her to be with me no matter what I am doing. I project my feelings onto her and therefore do things like buying a pickup and camper shell, going to the river or taking a run. I might tell myself all this is for her, but truly, it is what I want. It is hard to see that I bought an $18,000 dog house on wheels for me.

Perhaps projection will make more sense clarified from this perspective: Suppose you are visiting with a friend who comments that you seem "hyper." As you look inside to your own experience, you, in fact, feel reflective and withdrawn! Who do you suppose is feeling "hyper?" Be attentive to who says the words. The person saying the words is the person having or judging the experience. The words coming your way from another person may not be your experience to deal with. You can certainly consider someone's comments or feedback and then look inside to see what is going on with you. However, you do not have to own another person's experience that is projected upon you.

With projection in mind, go back and read aloud what you wrote about the flowers. As you read, become aware of any arising emotions (joy, sadness, etc.) or physical sensations (tight throat, laughter, tears, etc.) that occur. Pay attention to parts of your writing that cause emotion or physical sensation to arise.

QUESTIONS ABOUT THIS SESSION:

- What emotions and / or physical sensations arose in you as you read your writing?

- Where can you see yourself in what you have written? Go through it line by line. Look for general themes; look for specifics.

- How does what you have written reveal what you are feeling or thinking lately about things happening in your life?

- How do you suppose you *knew* what was going on with those flowers?

- If you discover that you feel resistant to accepting that you have these same qualities and issues, write about your resistance now. Why would you not want to accept that you have these qualities?

Here is what someone else wrote during the exercise with the flowers:

> "As I stand here, looking out, being observed by women in the group, my sense of self-consciousness is lessened by the awareness of other stems and blossoms that accompany me in this pathway. I am not the largest of flowers, or as grand as the rose perhaps, but my pastels and gentle presence are pleasing to me. I can't really see or touch all the others in this vase, but I'm aware of their presence and of my position as an object of awareness..."

How different is the above writing from yours? See if you can get any sense of what this writer is experiencing...make notes below:

Go back and read what you wrote about the flowers again. Any new insights? Be sure to record any new awareness before you end this first session.

END SESSION ONE

SESSION TWO

Here is what you will need to complete this session:
- 45 minutes of uninterrupted time
- Pages 9-11 of this workbook
- Something with which to write

Centering Yourself: Play the second centering exercise on the centering tape, following the suggestions given. Then write down any realizations and awarenesses you had while doing the centering.

An exercise to keep you focused on projection:
Study the picture below. Look carefully at the figure you see; then, in the following space, write what this person is feeling, thinking and experiencing. Yes, you are projecting, and now you get to watch yourself do it!

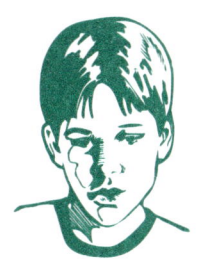

Rewrite the above work substituting "I", "me" and "my" every time you referred to the boy in the picture.

Now, read your new writing aloud.

Questions for you to consider:

- What insights come to you as you read over your writing?

- What issues, beliefs and concerns of yours are revealed?

- Had you seen these about yourself before?

END SESSION TWO

SESSION THREE

Here is what you will need to complete this session:
- 45 minutes of uninterrupted time
- Pages 12-13 of this workbook
- Something with which to write

Centering Yourself: Play the third centering exercise on the centering tape, following the suggestions given. Then write down any realizations and awarenesses you had while doing the centering.

Another Projection exercise:
Choose any stuffed toy animal or a real pet. Observe it for a minute or so. In the space below, write what it is like being this animal using third person pronouns (she, he, it).

Rewrite your observations below, substituting first person pronouns (I, me, and my) for any names or third person pronouns in your first writing.

Questions to consider:

• What insights come to you as you read over your writing? What issues, beliefs and concerns are revealed? Had you seen these about yourself before?

END SESSION THREE

SESSION FOUR

Here is what you will need to complete this session:
- 1-2 hours of uninterrupted time
- Pages 14-15 of this workbook
- Something with which to write

Centering Yourself: Play the fourth centering exercise on the centering tape, following the suggestions given. Then write down any realizations and awarenesses you had while doing the centering.

Yet another Projection exercise:
   Walk or drive to some place, like a shopping center or grocery store, where you can be around and observe strangers without feeling conspicuous. Spend a few minutes quietly, inconspicuously observing someone, allowing yourself to have an internal monologue about what is going on with this person you are watching.

   Go to a cafe (or home) where you can sit quietly; write down your observations of this person in the space below.

Now rewrite your words, substituting "I", "me" and "my" for the pronouns you used in the above writing.

Questions to consider: What have you revealed about yourself in this exercise? What insights come to you as you read over your writing? What issues, beliefs and concerns are revealed? Had you seen these about yourself before?

END SESSION FOUR

SESSION FIVE

Here is what you will need to complete this session:
- 1 hour of uninterrupted time
- Page 16 of this workbook
- Something with which to write

Centering Yourself: Play the fifth centering exercise on the centering tape, following the suggestions given. Then write down any realizations and awarenesses you had while doing the centering.

Projection Exercise:
Tell a friend about projection, this introspective skill you are learning and practicing. Share your earlier writing about the flowers with this friend. Ask your friend to share insights about you from your writing that you may have overlooked. When you are alone write about this experience of sharing below. Be aware of what you might be projecting onto your friend; *see if you can sort out what you know from what you might be projecting.*

END SESSION FIVE

SESSION SIX

Here is what you will need to complete this session:
- 1-2 hours of uninterrupted time
- Page 17 of this workbook
- Something with which to write

Centering Yourself: Play the sixth centering exercise on the centering tape, following the suggestions given. Then write down any realizations and awarenesses you had while doing the centering.

Projection Exercise:
Invite the friend you told about projection to go to the shopping center or grocery store with you. This time both of you inconspicuously observe (the same) someone, allowing your own internal monologues. When the two of you are alone, share your projections with each other. Then own your projections by discussing how the particulars you each *saw* in the stranger are actually going on in each of you.

When you are alone, write about this experience.

END SESSION SIX

SESSION SEVEN

Here is what you will need to complete this session:
- 1/2 hour of uninterrupted time
- Pages 18-20 of this workbook
- Something with which to write

Centering Yourself: Play the seventh centering exercise on the centering tape, following the suggestions given. Then write down any realizations and awarenesses you had while doing the centering.

Maybe you would like to take the day off today. If you want more words about projection, you are welcome to read these next few paragraphs. If more words do not work for you, start on Chapter 2 tomorrow.

By now you are realizing that whenever you observe something outside yourself - a picture, an object, someone's behavior, an interaction, etc. - you are projecting from your own inner experience of yourself. Even when we know that we are projecting, this does not stop us from doing it. Until now, you might have thought the only time people project is as they take a Rorschach test - that somehow we project onto the ink blot when asked, yet we do not project at other times. What is suggested here is this: WE PROJECT ALL THE TIME. Projection is how humans interpret, interact with, and externalize current-moment experiences. Freedom comes in being aware of this ongoing process. When we can know our current-moment experience, we stop projecting our perceptions, qualities and discriminations on others; we stop labeling and interpreting and judging other people's behavior.

If you say, "So-and-so is a jerk," it may not mean you are being a jerk toward someone in that moment (although you might consider that labeling someone a jerk is jerk-like behavior). If you are honest with yourself, you will realize that somewhere inside you know how to be, and have been, a jerk. You went to your own 'jerk' experience before labeling the other person's. This is where we can change ourselves - at this level of our conditioned self. If we are aware of ourselves labeling another person, thinking we know what is going on with them, we can take a breath and stop reacting to our projections. Now our choices are many: we can leave; we can ask the person what is going on with him or her; we can continue watching this person's behavior; we can have a rewarding internal monologue about what we have seen about ourselves.

There are not too many people who comprehend projection or even want to. Many people want or need to think they know what is going on with other people. Perhaps they derive a sense of control or comfort or safety in thinking they can detect what is going on with others. Perhaps this kind of thinking eases their fears. Why (do you project) might people not want to know about projection?

Here are several examples that suggest an understanding of projection:

"A loving person lives in a loving world; a hostile person lives in a hostile world. **Everyone you meet is your mirror.**" (*Wellness Book*)

"Projections are unclaimed self-perceptions." (Angeles Arrier, *The Four-Fold Way*)

"Nobody can do anything to me that I'm not already doing to myself." (Eleanor Roosevelt)

"Don't ever change the way you are,
'Cause I have a tendency
**To try and make you more
Of what I hope to be.**" (sung by Gloria Loring)

"...When we open our mouths to describe what we see, we in effect describe ourselves, our perceptions, our paradigms." (Covey, *Seven Habits of Highly Effective People*)

At the heart of understanding projection is accepting the awareness that we are experiencing the perceptions we have about people, events and situations. What we are seeing out there is what we are doing inside. *Accepting this awareness means accepting responsibility for how we react to others.* Sometimes it is not easy to acknowledge that the difficulty we have with others is only a reflection of the difficulty we have with some aspect of ourselves. Sometimes it is not easy or pleasant to recognize we are always looking into a mirror.

Let us say you are having a particular difficulty with a "problem" person in your life, say a girl friend. You find yourself criticizing her - her problem, her behavior; perhaps you find yourself talking about her to anyone who will listen. This is not to say she does not have this problem or these characteristics. But pause for a moment and ask yourself, "How is it that I *see* these things so plainly in someone outside myself?" Imagine your friend holding a mirror up in front of herself so you are seeing your own reflection. As you share your perceptions of what is "wrong" with her, you might recognize a part of yourself you have never seen before.

If you are like me and many others, your awareness of some internal aspects of yourself might be accompanied with judgment, embarrassment or shame. Sometimes it feels like I catch myself with my own hand in the cookie jar. Then I berate myself for what I have seen.

I urge you to not judge yourself as you continue to discover aspects of yourself throughout this workbook. When we judge ourselves, the aspect just revealed wants to hide and protect itself from the judgment.

Create for yourself a loving, accepting phrase, expressing gratitude to yourself for revealing any and every aspect of your inner world. Write that phrase below. Every time you discover anything about yourself, speak this phrase out loud, as often as you need. Maybe you can mark this page in the workbook. Any time you are being hard on yourself, you can quickly turn here, read these supportive words, and move away from being hard on yourself.

> A man who is seeking for realization is not only going round searching for his spectacles without realizing that they are on his nose all the time, but also were he not actually looking through them he would not be able to see what he is looking for!
>
> His only trouble is not knowing that they are there, and that alone hinders him from looking in the right direction. But the right direction is not without, for realization can never be an object of vision. The spectacles in question are mirrors that reflect the subject that is looking for itself.
>
> Terence Gray
> *Ask the Awakened*, 1973

END SESSION SEVEN

Centering

INTERIM SESSION ON CENTERING

Centering Yourself: Rewind the centering tape. Play the first centering exercise on the centering tape, following the suggestions given. Then write down any realizations and awarenesses you had while doing the centering.

Here are several questions to help recall your experience with centering over the past seven sessions: *Be thoughtful, take all the time you need, and record your responses.*

- What has been significant for you as you have participated in the centering exercises?

- What aspects of centering have you found easy? What parts are you drawn to? What do you like about centering?

- What aspects of centering have you found difficult? What parts are you not drawn to? What do you not like about centering?

- As you have probably noticed, the centering exercises teach you to be attentive to your body, your feelings or emotions and your mind. Which of these areas are you most aware of? Which do you find more difficult to access?

END INTERIM SESSION

Chapter 2

Postures

SESSION EIGHT

Here is what you will need to complete this session:
- 1 hour of uninterrupted time
- Pages 25-31 of this workbook
- Something with which to write

Centering Yourself: Play the second centering exercise on the centering tape, following the suggestions given. Then write down any realizations and awarenesses you had while doing the centering.

First Postures Exercise: *Postures Exposé*

Here is a Postures Exposé for you to take. You cannot fail this, for there are no right or wrong answers. In making a statement about each topic, you will have the opportunity to find a position, a belief - a posture - you have on the topic.

Write a simple statement about each topic, using the first thoughts that come to you:

Television and Violence

Strong women

Alcohol and drug abstinence

Senility

The Rain Forests

Date Rape

Postures

Sensitive men

Psychic Healers

AIDS

Meditation

   In the spaces below, write about your experience in doing the Postures Exposé. You might consider these questions:

• For which topics did your postures come easily?

- Which topics were difficult?

- Do you have several postures about any of the topics? Which ones?

- Were you reluctant to write down your postures? Could you get any sense of why you were reluctant?

- How do the statements you have written reveal postures you hold about these issues?

- Which of these postures could you share with a friend? What would keep you from sharing these postures?

Select three of your statements from the Postures Exposé and write the *opposite* of your posture in the following space.

Could you believe in and live by the statement you have just written? Why or why not? Do you know others who do believe the statement you have written? How do you feel toward them?

Which of the statements on the Postures Exposé seem *core* or *essential* to your belief system? Does this mean there are some you could let go of easily? Which one(s)? What new beliefs might replace them?

This second introspective process I call POSTULATION, or postures, for short. Viewed from out in the Universe, our world is one of dualities - diversities and extremes with degrees of variation in between. An example is black on one end, white on the other, and every shade between these two. When we grasp on to any one shade, and postulate that "This shade is good, right, and beautiful", we imply that the other variations are other than good, right and beautiful. We are postured. Once we are postured, it becomes very difficult to accept any other shade.

Now substitute 'issues' in place of simple colors. Once we grasp on to any side of an issue, and postulate that "This one is good, right, correct, etc.", we imply the other aspects of the issue are other than good, right and correct. We are postured. Once we are postured, it becomes very difficult to see any other side. Yet, is Greenpeace always right and the industrialist always wrong, or are there many sides to the issues? Were the Crusades a spiritual quest, a political expedient, or elements of each? Is it true that only two parents can make a stable family, or can a single parent create a loving, stable environment for raising children?

Anywhere we set ourselves on any continuum, we are establishing a posture. In the moment of attachment, we abandon our internal, authentic experience of unity and oneness. We then construct a life to support our postures. We raise our children to perpetuate our postures. We surround ourselves with a social network postured in ways similar to ours. And we tend our postures with great care, ignoring our deeper knowledge that all possibilities coexist.

Postures are present on many levels of our lives, and we are compelled to maintain, reinforce and defend them. Inclusively, they constitute our value system. Here are a few of the areas in which we might hold postures: what is good and what is bad behavior; how we should be treated; how we should treat others (this varies, of course, for friends, lovers, neighbors, earthlings, etc.); what is intimate and what is not; whether plants "feel"; whether we should lend money to friends; etc.

Postures by themselves are not *right* or *wrong*. One person's postures are not more right or wrong than another person's. Yet, for every posture we maintain or cling to, we create for ourselves a corresponding potential for suffering. Suffering means not getting what you want, getting what you want and not being satisfied, not being with those you love and enduring the company of those you do not love.

Suppose your posture is this: if you are in a committed relationship, then you and your partner should live together. One day your partner's employer assigns her a start-up project three states away where she will live for 8-10 months. If you cannot *loosen* your posture, if you cannot let yourself adjust to *what is* rather than what your posture dictates *should be*, then you suffer. You pout, withdraw, or end the relationship. In not recognizing and letting go of your posture, you actually cause your own suffering. The holding on is the problem - not the posture itself. Can you see this?

Second Postures Exercise: *Postures and Suffering*

• Think of a time in your recent past when you were suffering (unhappy, miserable). Recall the details of that time as fully as you can, and write them down in the following space.

- Now write down what you think *should* have happened in that situation - what you wanted to happen.

- Write out the postures you have just discovered; write how holding on to these postures caused you suffering.

    Postures are the emotional, mental and physical filters that affect what we see in our experiences. As you continue to look inward, you will discover how postures are the stances from which you project what you postulate is going on in your world. As with projection, the place where something is going on is inside of you - not necessarily "out there" in the world.

    The introspective work related to postures is first awareness, then acceptance of these postures as they arise within us. Only with awareness and acceptance do we have the opportunity to watch their potential to influence us, while choosing not to let that happen. Or perhaps we will just watch how we behave under the influence of a particular posture. If our posture truly gets in our way, we could remove ourselves from the situation, or consider reevaluating the posture.

END SESSION EIGHT

SESSION NINE

Here is what you will need to complete this session:
- 1 hour of uninterrupted time
- Pages 32-37 of this workbook
- Something with which to write

Centering Yourself: Play the third centering exercise on the centering tape, following the suggestions given. Then write down any realizations and awarenesses you had while doing the centering.

Another Postures Exercise: *Levels and Degrees of Postures*

As we mentioned before, we use the term *postures* to mean the standards, principles, beliefs, attitudes and opinions we were taught as children and continue to hold now as adults. We hold on to our postures with varying degrees of intensity, directly correlated to our feeling of how essentially they define who we are.

Following the examples below, write out your postures according to the classifications as defined.

1. Write down a STANDARD you have. A standard is a measure of quality. Ex: I will not eat green bananas.

2. Write down a PRINCIPLE you have. A principle is a governing law of conduct. Ex: I don't say something about a person that I can't say to him.

3. Write down a BELIEF you have. A belief is trust or confidence in some person or thing. Ex: All women can assert themselves clearly.

4. Write down an ATTITUDE you have. An attitude is a disposition grounded in affect and emotion. Ex: No matter who calls, I rarely like to talk on the phone.

5. Write down an OPINION you have. An opinion is a view formed in the mind about a particular matter. Ex: Computer wizards are geeks.

Postures Identification Exercise. From the following groups, circle the terms with which you identify.

reactionary
terrorist
rightist
radical
leftist

liberal
moderate
conservative
autocrat
totalitarian
dictatorial

ordinary
normal
average

male
female
transsexual

southern
northern
mid-western
Californian
Texan
southwestern
northwestern

city person
country person

upper class
middle class
lower class

drinker
non-drinker

short hair
no hair
long hair

straight
homosexual
gay
bi-sexual
asexual
heterosexual

introvert
extrovert
socializer
recluse
intellectual

working class
professional
student
artist
conservationist

dog person
cat person

american car driver
foreign car driver

occidental
Hispanic
African-American
native American
Asian

omnivore
carnivore
vegetarian
lacto-vegetarian

independent
Republican
Democrat
communist
socialist
libertarian

Muslim
Hindu
Catholic
Christian
Buddhist
Jewish
atheist
agnostic

assertive
passive
sophisticated
aggressive
naive

father
mother
husband
wife
youth
breadwinner

smoker
ex-smoker
non-smoker

old-fashioned
modern
macho
feminist
cross-dresser

Some of us fiercely resist labeling ourselves, as we are asked to do in the above exercise. Yet, in truth, there are distinguishing ways to describe each of us that set us apart from one another, and there are beliefs, principles and values accompanying these differences.

As if you were introducing yourself to a new person, write a descriptive sentence in the following space using all the *terms* you selected on page 34 and any other labels or characteristics you would like.

"I am a

You might want or need to journal here about your experience in writing this description.

Could you telephone someone right this minute and read this self-introduction to him or her? Write down below the name(s) of the person(s) you could call.

To which close family member could you read your self-description? Could you call your best friend? Go ahead, call someone...and pay close attention to all that arises within you as you read this description to someone. Do you leave any phrases out? Are some harder to own than others? Make notes about your experience in the following space.

Further Postures Insights:

Suppose you heard a woman read this self-introduction:

> I am a southern democrat; a gay professional; a liberal - radical, country person who loves cats and dogs; an expensive foreign car driver with short blond hair; a self-made millionaire female buddhist; an assertive feminist extrovert.

Take a few minutes to write your thoughts, feelings and reactions about this woman. Would you like to meet her? How might the two of you get along? Which of your postures would clash with hers? Might you be friends? Or would you avoid one another?

Single out one description of this woman that you find particularly unappealing and let yourself launch into ranting and raving about "people who are like this". How do you feel about people who are like this? Why shouldn't she be this way? Why is she *wrong* to be this way? How should she be? *Be honest here; nobody will see it except you.*

Let yourself write out in detail the behaviors and attitudes (your postures) you must maintain in order to continue to feel the way you do about the woman.

Suppose this woman were your daughter or sister. How would you modify your postures or make exceptions for her? How would you reconcile your postures with your relationship with her? Would any of your postures keep you from having a loving relationship with your own kin? Can you have a fully open heart with someone whose postures differ from yours?

One way we maintain our identity is by opposing persons with differing postures. It is as if we do not know who we are; we know who we are not. You see, if you were solid in your recognition and acceptance of who or how you are, there would be no need to hold any posture or opinion about anyone else. How they are would not stimulate any reaction in you.

END SESSION NINE

SESSION TEN

Here is what you will need to complete this session:
- 1 hour of uninterrupted time
- Pages 38-41 of this workbook
- Something with which to write

Centering Yourself: Play the fourth centering exercise on the centering tape, following the suggestions given. Then write down any realizations and awarenesses you had while doing the centering.

Postures Exercise: *Major Messages*

Can you think of a major message you received about yourself as a child? This message may have been verbal or nonverbal. It was probably from a significant adult like your parent(s), grandparent(s), aunt, uncle, brother or sister, or an early grade school teacher. This message would have pertained to how you behaved or how you were as a being; it could have felt positive or negative to you. If you remember several, write them all down in the space below. Then, draw a circle around the one you will use in this exercise. Take as much time as you need to remember these messages.

Rewrite this major message as an "I" statement. It might look like this: "I am a pest when I want attention." Or "I'm not very smart, but I surely am strong." Or "I'll go far someday." Or "I'm too emotional."

Rewrite your major message here in the space provided. Then say it out loud.

After you have completed the task above, read the following description of the activity you have been doing. It might be helpful to read it several times.

We create postures within our emotional, mental and physical aspects as we adjust to the major messages (verbal and nonverbal) we received as children. Postures are the values, standards, beliefs and attitudes we learn as part of our early childhood conditioning. Sometimes they are intentionally taught to us. Other times we just pick them up. Usually we have not chosen these postures freely as adults.

When we are very young, we are given many messages about who and what we are, how we should and should not be, what is OK and what is not OK, what is Right and what is Wrong. These messages are given with the implication that our acceptance of them is directly related to our emotional - and often our physical - survival. Love and safety are withheld if we do not adjust to this message. Receiving this message often enough, we eventually realize our survival is at stake. So we wisely incorporate the message into our belief system of who and how we are. Some of us own the message and become what we are told. Some of us, in our steadfast refusal to own the message, assume an opposite posture. Either way, eventually we adjust to someone else's perception rather than our own experience (about ourselves, about others, about the world, about ethnic groups, etc.). Then we work at maintaining these postures by adhering to them strongly and giving them to others. We project from these postures, imposing our conditioned structure on other people, usually as "I do...and you should too..."

See if you can put your major message into the "You should..." or "You should not..." admonition you may have found yourself giving to others. If you bought into the posture, you probably give others a "You should..." If you rejected the posture, you probably feel others "should not..." Change your "I" message (from p. 39) to a "You" message.

The major messages we cited earlier (p. 39) might become:

You should not be a pest. OR You should not need attention.

Now write your major message projected as a posture of how others should be:

You should or should not

Read this changed message out loud once or twice. Imagine yourself giving your best friend this message. Say it out loud, putting your best friend's name first in your sentence.

Perhaps we bite our tongues to keep from speaking these postures out loud. Yet they are here inside us, forming the structure of who we think we (and others) are, and how we think we (and others) should behave. Actually, 'shoulds', 'oughts', and 'should nots' or 'ought nots' are perfect clues that postures have been expressed. Since the structure of our identity is nothing more solid and *real* than postures, and since we do not want to see the insecurity of our identity, we think our postures become more valid if we can convince others our postures are the *right* ones. We work at getting others to believe as we do. We eliminate people from our lives whose postures differ from ours, for to admit another's postures are valid might mean our postures are wrong and we might have to change. And we do not want to change.

When we grow up, we define ourselves by our postures. See how easily you can complete these phrases:

I am a person who

I believe in

A *good* person does these things:

A *bad* person does these things:

   Most of us will expend considerable energy and effort defending our postures. Ultimately, couples divorce, families divide, communities put up fences and countries fight wars over holding onto postures.

> As far back as Chuang-tse we find the story of the old monk who, in despair of knowing enlightenment before he died, went to Lao-tse. On arrival Lao-tse came out to meet him, welcomed him, but told him to leave his followers and his baggage outside the gate, for otherwise he would not be admitted. The old man had no followers, and no baggage, but he understood, went in and found his fulfillment.
>
>   Terence Gray
>   *Ask the Awakened*, 1973

END SESSION TEN

INTERIM SESSION ON CENTERING

Centering Yourself: Play the fifth centering exercise on the centering tape, following the suggestions given. Then write down any realizations and awarenesses you had while doing the centering.

Here are several questions to help recall your experience with centering over the last four sessions: *Be thoughtful, take all the time you need, and record your responses.*

- What has been significant for you as you have participated in the centering exercises?

- What aspects of centering have you found easy? To which parts are you drawn? What do you like about centering?

- What aspect of centering have you found difficult? What parts are you not drawn to? What do you not like about centering?

- As you have probably noticed, the centering exercises guide you through being attentive to your body, your feelings or emotions and your mind. Of which of these areas are you most aware? Which do you find more difficult to access?

END INTERIM SESSION

Chapter 3

Subpersonalities

SESSION ELEVEN

Here is what you will need to complete this exercise:
- 1 hour of uninterrupted time
- Pages 45-51 of this workbook
- Something with which to write

Centering Yourself: Play the sixth centering exercise on the centering tape, following the suggestions given. Then write down any realizations and awarenesses you had while doing the centering.

Discovering several Subpersonalities: Write down three major events or activities from your day (or from yesterday). Choose three different things, not several from the same category of activities. For instance:

I meditated.

    I ran 5 miles.

        I called my mother.

           I worked on the book I'm writing.

Write your three activities on these lines.

_____

_____

_____

Select one of your activities to focus on first. Close your eyes and imagine yourself participating in the activity. Recall as much of your actual experience as you can. In your mind's eye, see yourself participating in this activity as clearly as you can. How are you behaving? What thoughts are in your mind? What feelings and emotions do you experience during this activity? How are you dressed?

When you have visualized as much as you can for now, write down in the spaces below what you discovered in this imagery:

Thoughts:

Feelings / Emotions:

Behaviors:

Dress:

Think of the circle above as the head on a body. Can you add a trunk, arms, hands, legs and feet to express the activity you saw in your imagery? Simple stick drawings are fine! Can you add facial features that are expressive of the image of yourself you saw in your mind's eye?

What would you name this part of yourself? _____

Select a second of your activities from page 45 to focus on. Close your eyes and imagine yourself participating in the activity. Recall as much of your actual experience as you can. In your mind's eye, see yourself participating in this activity as clearly as you can. How are you behaving? What thoughts are in your mind? What feelings and emotions do you experience during this activity? How are you dressed?

When you have visualized as much as you can for now, write down in the spaces below what you discovered in this imagery:

Thoughts:

Feelings / Emotions:

Behaviors:

Dress:

Think of the circle above as the head on a body. Can you add a trunk, arms, hands, legs and feet to express the activity you saw in your imagery? Simple stick drawings are fine! Now, can you add facial features that are expressive of the image of yourself you saw in your mind's eye?

What would you name this part of yourself? _____

Now, do this same process with the third activity you wrote down on page 45. Close your eyes and imagine yourself participating in the activity. Recall as much of your actual experience as you can. In your mind's eye, see yourself participating in this activity as clearly as you can. How are you behaving? What thoughts are in your mind? What feelings and emotions do you experience during this activity? How are you dressed?

When you have visualized as much as you can for now, write down in the spaces below what you discovered in this imagery:

How do you talk to yourself?

What do you feel?

How do you behave?

Do you wear any special clothing?

Think of the circle above as the head on a body. Can you add a trunk, arms, hands, legs and feet to express the activity you saw in your imagery? Simple stick drawings are fine! Can you add facial features that are expressive of the image of yourself you saw in your mind's eye?

What would you name this part of yourself? _____

Take a few moments to review the last three pages of your notebook, looking carefully and fully at the drawings you have made. Using the circles below as "heads", draw each of the figures you created on pages 46-48.

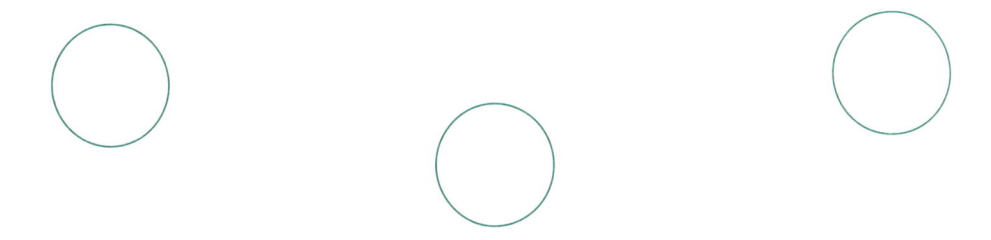

In responding to the questions below, you will discover how these three parts of you are alike and different.

- How are the three body postures alike / different?

- Which use hands...feet...head...etc?

- Which interact with others?

- Which ones have significant feeling or emotion accompanying them?

- In which ones are your energy and attention focused in your head?

- Would the dress of any one of them be appropriate for another one? Which? If not, why not?

In completing the last five pages, you have discovered three of your SUBPERSONALITIES. We say 'subpersonality' because you are not any one of these parts of yourself all the time. Since none of these three is your total personality, each unique aspect is a 'sub' personality.

There are several essential concepts to comprehend about subpersonalities if we are to use them as a tool of introspection. I recommend two books that provide much more detail than I will present here. *What We May Be* by Louis Ferrucci and *The Unfolding Self* by Molly Young Brown both offer explanation and exercises to deepen groundedness in this process.

We are taught to refer to ourselves as "I". No matter that there might be extreme changes, even reversals in our thoughts, feelings and behaviors from one minute to another, we are taught to use the language of "I". From referring to ourselves with this single word, we come to experience ourselves as singular, as indivisible with a monolithic quality. Yet when I look more closely I discover that the part of me who calls my mother is not the same part of me who goes for a 5-mile run. Each of these aspects of me is motivated quite differently, has very different needs, and has postures and views of the world that the other part does not hold. Subpersonalities are like friends who generally share the same values, yet differ in how they manifest those values in their lives. The part who calls my mother has the need to be loved, to feel connected, to be respectful of someone she loves and honors. The Runner in me needs to be healthy and fit; she is afraid to not keep her heart strong; and she loves the activity of running. If the Runner called my mother and talked about fitness and running, my mother might well wonder who was talking to her!

Some mornings there can be an internal struggle between the Runner and the Bookwriter. Each of these two parts of me has legitimate needs, and will push internally to have its needs met.

The Runner says things like: "Now's the time! This is the coolest part of the day. If we're going to get in a 45-minute run, we'd better go now. Once we start on the rest of the day, it'll be hard to break the routine and go for a run."

The Bookwriter says, with great enthusiasm: "Now is when my energy is best. Meditation has left me quiet and clear. Let's go finish the section on centering we started yesterday."

Runner counters, "Come on! You know I can't run in the heat. You can work on the book later when you're back inside the house where it's cool. But I have to be outside to run!" Panic is rising in her voice.

Bookwriter, upping her ante, offers, "But I need..."

Can you hear how each of the parts of me can make a good case? Depending upon which of these subpersonalities succeeds in getting its needs met, "I" play the corresponding role. "I" run or "I" write. And as I play one role, the other subpersonality is not getting its needs met; its needs, perceptions, and postures are cut off from my awareness. "I" identify with - "I" become the Runner. Bookwriter's needs are lost to me for the time being.

Every one of our subpersonalities is essential to us. Each one has qualities, perceptions, and experiences that are essential to our uniqueness and to our well-being. Each holds our well-being as the reason it exists. Each knows within itself that it exists to promote and maintain our well-being. You may find that in your initial discovery of a subpersonality, you are unable to see aspects of it that have your best interests at heart. Yet upon examination, you will find that those aspects are there.

There is a working process we can apply internally which allows us to harmonize our multitude of subpersonalities. These five steps, generally occurring sequentially, are:

> RECOGNITION - we recognize or become aware of the various parts of ourselves.
>
> ACCEPTANCE - we fully acknowledge and embrace these parts of ourselves without any judgement.
>
> COORDINATION - With practice in staying centered, we coordinate the needs, energies, and qualities of the many subpersonalities within ourselves, facilitating their becoming cooperative rather than competitive.
>
> INTEGRATION - With continued stepping back, we are able to choose the qualities and energies we want to manifest in given situations.
>
> SYNTHESIS - As our growth moves us toward transpersonal experiences, the masks of the personal self gently dissolve and we realize universal oneness. Some would say we experience God. Some say we realize All That Is. Ancient seekers used the Sanskrit words *Sat-Chit-Ananda* (being-consciousness-bliss) or *Nirvana* (extinction).

Just for a second, can you let yourself experience no layers of the personal self?

END SESSION ELEVEN

SESSION TWELVE

Here is what you will need to complete this session:
- 1 hour of uninterrupted time
- The provided tape
- Pages 52-55 of this workbook
- Something with which to write

Centering Yourself: The centering for Session 12 is the first part of the guided imagery for this subpersonality exercise. Both the centering and the exercise are on side 2 of the tape accompanying this workbook.

Another exercise on subpersonalities: *The Bus*

Listen to the first guided imagery on side 2 of the tape. Then write out your experience in the following space.

When you have finished writing *The Bus* imagery, respond to these questions:

• Which subpersonality did you feel drawn to relate to? Is this the one you did relate to in the exercise?

• Was this subpersonality paired with another? How did you handle this in your imagery?

• Describe the subpersonality - its age, clothes, body posture, behaviors, facial expressions, etc.

• What is this subpersonality's name?

• What are your initial feelings toward this subpersonality?

- What does this subpersonality want from you? What does it need?

- How does the world look through the eyes of this subpersonality?

- What would your life be like if you were this subpersonality all of the time?

- Write honestly here what you like and dislike about this subpersonality.

- How could the two of you relate together better?

- Who was driving the bus? What are the qualities and characteristics of the bus driver?

- When you went onto the bus, was a subpersonality still on it? Describe in detail any interaction you had with this subpersonality.

Make any other notes about this exercise that seem relevant to you:

END SESSION TWELVE

SESSION THIRTEEN

Here is what you will need to complete this session:
- 1 hour uninterrupted time
- The provided tape
- Pages 56-59 of this workbook
- Something with which to write

Centering Yourself: The centering for Session 13 is the first part of the guided imagery for this subpersonality exercise. Both the centering and the exercise are on side 2 of the tape accompanying this workbook.

Another Exercise on subpersonalities: *Alone on a Hill*
Listen to the second guided imagery on side 2 of the tape. Then write out your experience in the following space.

When you have finished writing out the *Alone on a Hill* imagery, respond to these questions:

• Describe how you felt when you were first alone on the hilltop.

• What was your reaction to seeing yourself as the small child coming up the hill?

• Describe your interaction with the small child.

• How accepting are you of this part of yourself? What steps on your part would develop more acceptance?

- What was your reaction to seeing your judging self coming up the hill?

- Describe your interaction with the *Judge*.

- How accepting are you of this part of yourself that judges? What steps on your part would develop more acceptance?

- What was your reaction to seeing an emotional part of yourself coming up the hill?

- Describe your interaction with the emotion.

- How accepting are you of this emotion? What steps on your part would develop more acceptance?

- When the three subpersonalities were gone, who was left there on the hilltop? Describe the aspect of yourself that you saw remaining on the hill.

END SESSION THIRTEEN

SESSION FOURTEEN

Here is what you will need to complete this session:
- 1 hour of uninterrupted time
- Pages 60-65 of this workbook
- A cassette recorder and 60-minute blank tape

Centering Yourself: Set a watch or timer for 5 minutes. During that time focus on your in and out breaths, counting silently each time you exhale. When you have counted up to ten breaths, start counting again at one. When you catch your mind wandering, come back to focusing on the last number you remember. Make notes of your experience below.

Subpersonality Exercise: *Listening to your Subpersonalities*

Through the last three sessions you have begun to recognize and accept more than a few of your subpersonalities. In this next exercise, you will begin to know three subpersonalities more fully, by concentrating on their voices (what they sound like) and the postures each holds.

First, select three subpersonalities you feel you want to know more fully. As a guideline you might consider:
- one you feel resistance toward
- one you think behaves inappropriately (too needy, silly, angry, etc.)
- one you experience intense emotion toward
- one you know you need to embrace more completely
- one which confuses you

List below the three you have selected:

1)

2)

3)

Turn to the writing you entered in your workbook when you first met the subpersonality whose name is in the first slot above. Read what it shared with you, experiencing as fully as you can how it felt to be this subpersonality. Read its experience aloud into the tape recorder, using the first person "I", as if the subpersonality were talking. Let yourself become this subpersonality as you did in the previous imagery. When you reach the end of the reading, close your eyes and let this subpersonality continue to talk as long, as completely, as fully as it wants. If you come to a silence, gently prompt the subpersonality to continue talking. You might say, "I'd like to hear more", or "What else do you want to say about that?" Keep yourself open to listening, and speak out loud whatever this subpersonality wants to say. When you feel all talking is over for now, turn off the tape recorder. Take several full, deep breaths; get up and move around a little; maybe stretch.

Rewind the tape. With this workbook close by, listen to the tape you have just made, making notes in the space below of significant realizations. Write about the tone of this subpersonality's voice. Be sure to write down key words or phrases that are repeated several times. Can you identify the beliefs, values and postures of this subpersonality?

Now turn to the writing you entered in your workbook when you first met the subpersonality whose name is in the second slot above. Read what it shared with you, experiencing as fully as you can how it felt to be this subpersonality. Read its experience aloud into the tape recorder, using the first person "I", as if the subpersonality were talking. Let yourself become this subpersonality as you did in the previous imagery. When you reach the end of the reading, close your eyes and let this subpersonality continue to talk as long, as completely, as fully as it wants. If you come to a silence, gently prompt the subpersonality to continue talking. You might say, "I'd like to hear more", or "What else do you want to say about that?" Keep yourself open to listening, and speak aloud whatever this subpersonality wants to say. When you feel all talking is over for now, turn off the tape recorder. Take several full, deep breaths; get up and move around a little; maybe stretch.

Rewind the tape. With this workbook close by, listen to the tape you have just made, making notes in the space below of significant realizations. Write about the tone of this subpersonality's voice. Be sure to write down key words or phrases that are repeated several times. Can you identify the beliefs, values and postures of this subpersonality?

Now turn to the writing you entered in your workbook when you first met the subpersonality whose name is in the third slot above. Read what it shared with you, experiencing as fully as you can how it felt to be this subpersonality. Read its experience aloud into the tape recorder, using the first person "I", as if the subpersonality were talking. Let yourself become this subpersonality as you did in the previous imagery. When you reach the end of the reading, close your eyes and let this subpersonality continue to talk as long, as completely, as fully as it wants. If you come to a silence, gently prompt the subpersonality to continue talking. You might say, "I'd like to hear more", or "What else do you want to say about that?" Keep yourself open to listening, and speak aloud whatever this subpersonality wants to say. When you feel all talking is over for now, turn off the tape recorder. Take several full, deep breaths; get up and move around a little; maybe stretch.

Rewind the tape. With this workbook close by, listen to the tape you have just made, making notes in the space below of significant realizations. Write about the tone of this subpersonality's voice. Be sure to write down key words or phrases that are repeated several times. Can you identify the beliefs, values and postures of this subpersonality?

Rewind your tape to the very beginning of these three subpersonality monologues. Listen again, this time to all three, one right after another. Listen for differences you can hear as these parts of you talk.

- How are they different?

- How do their needs vary?

- Do any seem identified with logic, reason or rationality?

- Do any seem identified with feelings or emotions?

- Do these subpersonalities have any problem accepting each other? Are they conflicted?

- Do you have difficulty accepting any aspects of these three subpersonalities? Write out this difficulty now, and see if you can discover another subpersonality, the one who is contrary to - and therefore paired with - the part it is resisting.

> A myriad bubbles were floating on the surface of a stream. "What are you?" I cried to them as they drifted by. "I am a bubble, of course" nearly a myriad bubbles answered, and there was surprise and indignation in their voices as they passed. But, here and there, a lonely bubble answered, "We are this stream", and there was neither surprise nor indignation in their voices, but just a quiet certitude.
>
> Terence Gray
> *Ask the Awakened*, 1973

END SESSION FOURTEEN

INTERIM SESSION ON CENTERING

Here are several questions to help recall your experience with centering over the last three sessions: *Be thoughtful, take all the time you need, and record your responses.*

• What has been significant for you as you have participated in the centering exercises?

• What aspects of centering have you found easy? To which parts are you drawn? What do you like about centering?

- What aspects of centering have you found difficult? What parts are you not drawn to? What do you not like about centering?

- As you have probably noticed, the centering exercises teach you to be attentive to your body, your feelings or emotions and your mind. Of which of these areas are you most aware? Which do you find more difficult to access?

END INTERIM SESSION

Chapter 4

Disidentification

SESSION FIFTEEN

Here is what you will need to complete this session:
- 45 minutes of uninterrupted time
- Pages 69-72 of this workbook
- Something with which to write

Centering Yourself: The centering for Session 15 is the first part of the guided imagery for this disidentification exercise. Both the centering and the exercise are on side 2 of the tape accompanying this workbook, following Session 13, *Alone on a Hill*.

Disidentification Exercise: *Letting Go*

Listen to the *Letting Go* guided imagery on the tape. Then write out your experience in the following space.

When you have finished writing the *Letting Go* imagery, respond to the questions below :

- If you have not already done so, describe your experience of letting go.

- What keeps you from letting go?

- What is the form of the part of you that keeps you from letting go?

- Where does this part stay?

- How does this part keep you from letting go?

- What would your life be like if you did not respond to the part that keeps you from letting go?

Here are some important points to be made about DISIDENTIFICATION:

We can relate to a part (a subpersonality) of ourselves.

Until we become aware of the part, we are identified with it and dominated by its conditioned responses to its world.

When we can disidentify from the part (step away from and see it as an aspect of our conditioning), we are free to choose how we will respond.

Unconditioned consciousness takes on the form of whatever arises within it.

Have you ever listened to a friend relate an experience she endured that really upset her or made her angry? As you listened, you felt anger and indignation rising in yourself. This is "identifying". You can not help your friend because you are both now simmering in the same stew. There is no one left to turn off the stove.

It is as if you went to see a friend who was in bed sick. Rather than sitting beside the bed for your visit, you climbed on the bed and became sick alongside this friend. This is what we call "identifying with" something or someone. We take on the behaviors, feelings and beliefs of what we come in contact with, especially what arises within us. We give up being centered and focused within our own experience; we identify with an experience external to our center. We especially identify with and take on the experience of subpersonalities as they arise within us. One minute we are calm; the next we are judging something that is occurring around us.

Disidentification is the internal process of staying centered as we observe what arises within and around us. It helps to have a loving, gentle "Is that so?" attitude about oneself and others. Disidentification is stepping back away from your present moment experience to both have the experience and recognize that you are having the experience.

In case you are wondering if disidentification causes us to feel distant, the answer is no. That process is called detachment or disassociation, in which one removes oneself from one's internal and external experience and is absent to what is going on. With practice in disidentifying, you actually are present more, not less. Since you have not limited yourself by identifying with just one aspect, you are open to all; you are all.

It might be helpful to reread pages 29-30, 39-41 and 50-51 of your workbook. You will begin to discover that when you are identified with a posture or a subpersonality, that is the only view or perception available to you. All other qualities, truths, skills, and experiences are unavailable as long as you are identified with any limited aspect of self.

There is no judgement here; I hold no posture that you should have more of you available to you. I just want you to know how to be free.

END SESSION FIFTEEN

SESSION SIXTEEN

Here is what you will need to complete this session:
- 10 minutes to read the directions for the exercise
- A fairly quiet day for yourself (especially not much public interaction)
- Page 73 of your workbook, and something to write with
- Notify your family and friends that you will be doing this exercise

Centering Yourself: Set a watch or timer for 8 minutes. During that time, focus on your in and out breaths, counting each breath silently as you exhale. When you have counted up to ten breaths, start counting again at one. When you catch your mind wandering, come back to focusing on the last number you remember.

Disidentification Exercise: *Speaking in the Third Person*
For the rest of this day, until you go to bed tonight, in all your conversations or monologues, refer to yourself with an appropriate third person pronoun. If you are female, use "she", "hers" and "her" all the rest of the day. If you are male, use "he", "his" and "him" the rest of the day. When someone says, "Hi, how are you?", you will respond, "She's great [females], thanks for asking!" When someone says, "How do you feel about going out for dinner?", you will respond "He'd [males] like going out tonight. What a great idea!"

In every place you would usually use "I", "me" and "my", be attentive to using the third person pronoun. Be sure to set aside an hour or so for writing about this exercise at the end of the day. You will be amazed at what you will see. Write it all down in the following space.

END SESSION SIXTEEN

SESSION SEVENTEEN

Here is what you will need to complete this session:
- 1/2 hour uninterrupted time alone
- Pages 74-75 of this workbook
- 1 hour of assistance from a close friend
- Something with which to write

Centering Yourself: Set a watch or timer for 8 minutes. During that time, focus on your in and out breaths, counting each breath silently as you exhale. When you have counted up to ten breaths, start counting again at one. When you catch your mind wandering, come back to focusing on the last number you remember.

Disidenfitication Exercise: *And Then (S)He…*

First, recall an upsetting incident you have experienced recently that involved another person. (NOTE: Do not choose an incident involving the friend who will arrive shortly to assist you in this exercise. It just would not be appropriate right now.) Spend up to half an hour writing this incident in the space below as fully as you can remember. Specifically recall the exchanges of the incident: I did so-and-so; Roger said this-and-that; I responded this way; Roger upped the ante with that.

When your friend arrives to participate with you in this session, take a few moments to share all the instructions. Next, read to your friend exactly what you have written in your workbook.

Now read what you have written out loud to your friend again. This time use the third person pronouns (she, her, hers / he, him, his) for all references to YOURSELF. Continue using the other person's name throughout the reading.

Discuss with your friend any differences you experienced between the first and second variations in reading your incident. In particular, speak about how identified you were, or were not, in each reading. You will probably need to explain disidentification to your friend.

Make notes below about doing this exercise.

> It is not the eye that sees, it is not the ear that hears: there is seeing, there is hearing. Who sees? Who hears? *No one.* That is the truth. For the seeing and the seen, the hearing and the heard are impersonality, impersonal consciousness.
> Terence Gray
> *Ask the Awakened,* 1973

END SESSION SEVENTEEN

FINAL SESSION ON CENTERING

At this point, you have participated in 18 centering exercises, and you have those experiences within to draw upon in responding to these questions:

• What is your experience of being centered? What happens in your body, your feelings, and your mind?

• Can you write a definition of centering?

• How does being centered relate to or affect doing introspective work and using introspective skills?

> As you continue to watch the mind, the awareness deepens. And as the awareness deepens, more and more tapes lose energy, lose force, lose reality. More and more of them disappear. It is not that you are trying to make them disappear, no. There is an acceptance of them, you are perfectly willing to have them there. In that very awareness and acceptance, though, they start disappearing of their own accord. And as they start disappearing a great silence increasingly descends on you. You become more and more still within.
> James Sloman
> *Nothing*, 1981

END FINAL SESSION

Epilogue

What might you do now? Consider the wisdom in this simple verse:

> The world is round,
> and the place which may seem like the end
> may also be only the beginning.
>
> Ivy Baker Priest
> *Parade*, Feb. 16, 1958

GLOSSARY OF TERMS

Centering: being present to this moment and to whatever arises in it; not being pulled away from present moment awareness; attention focused in the present moment; "personal experience of non-attachment" (Brown, *The Unfolding Self*, 1983).

Disidentification: being aware of, yet not clinging to conditioned aspects of consciousness that arise; observing what is arising without becoming involved or attached.

Postures: any / all layers of conditioned response arising with stimulation (internal and external), including values, principles, beliefs, paradigms, standards, attitudes.

Projection: externalization of one's current-moment experience; ignoring and separating from internal experience and objectifying it outside; taking that which is intrinsic and making it extrinsic; "the attributing of one's internal characteristics or conflicts onto external people, objects, or events" (Brown, *The Unfolding Self*, 1983).

Subpersonalities: a role; a conditioned aspect of self distinguishable from other aspects in its needs, behaviors, and self-talk; "a semi-autonomous, structured constellation of attitudes, drives, habit patterns, logical elements which is organized in adaptation to forces in the internal and external environment" (Crampton, *Psychosynthesis: some key aspects of theory and practice*, 1977).

FURTHER READING

A Center for the Practice of Zen Buddhist Meditation (1984). *The Key: And the Name of the Key is Willingness*. Mt. View, CA.

A Center for the Practice of Zen Buddhist Meditation (1990). *That Which You Are Seeking Is Causing You To Seek*. Mt. View, CA.

Adair, Margo (1984). *Working Inside Out: Tools for Change*. Berkeley, CA: Wingbow Press.

Aitken, Robert (1982). *Taking the Path of Zen*. San Francisco: North Point Press.

Brown, Molly Young (1984). *The Unfolding Self*. Los Angeles: Psychosynthesis Press.

Chopra, Deepak (1993). *Ageless Body, Timeless Mind: The Quantum Alternative to Growing Old*. New York: Harmony Books.

Chopra, Deepak (1993). *Creating Affluence: Wealth Consciousness in the Field of All Possibilities*. San Rafael, CA: New World Library.

Covey, Stephen (1988). *Seven Habits of Highly Effective People*. New York: Simon & Schuster.

Ferrucci, Louis (1982). *What We May Be*. Los Angeles: Tarcher.

Gendlin, E. (1981). *Focusing*. Toronto: Bantam Press.

Gray, Terence (1973). *Ask the Awakened*. Boston: Little, Brown and Company.

Hendricks, G., & Wills, R. (1975). *The Centering Book*. New Jersey: Prentice-Hall, Inc.

Huber, Cheri (1993). *There Is Nothing Wrong With You*. Mt. View, CA: Keep It Simple Books.

Kennett, Roshi Jiyu (1976). *Zen Is Eternal Life*. Emeryville, CA: Dharma Press.

Nyanatiloka (1971). *The Word of the Buddha*. Kandy, Ceylon: Buddhist Publication Society.

Sloman, James (1981). *Nothing*. Durham, NC: Dana Institute.